by
Anna Blair

To Duncan, who is interested in old days and ways.

This photograph of Kilmarnock Road, facing south, was taken some time in the 1950s. Pelosi's Cafe (on the right) was already a local institution by the time the shops were added to its left in the mid-1930s. At some time, unnoticed, the low parapet which lent a little interesting architectural character to the terrace was removed.

© Anna Blair 2003
First published in the United Kingdom, 2003,
by Stenlake Publishing
Telephone / Fax: 01290 551122
Printed by Cordfall Ltd, Glasgow, G21 2QA

ISBN 1 84033 264 6

_he author's royalties from the sale of this book have been donated to Capability Scotland,
supporting children and adults in Scotland with a wide range of disabilities.

**The publishers regret that they cannot supply copies of any pictures featured in this book.
Copies of those pictures provided by East Renfrewshire Council (see acknowledgements), may be obtained by contacting Giffnock Library.**

ACKNOWLEDGEMENTS

This book would not have been produced without the help of many people, generous with their time, information and expertise. Warm thanks are due to all those who lent or processed the photographs in the collection, were able to identify features in them, verify historical details or permitted the use of their pictures. Among those are Margaret Black, Shirley Campbell, Jackson Cadaw, Gordon Davidson, James Dewar, Mary Gardner, Nan Gardner, Jack Greenshields, David Harvey, Lily Noble, Alan Perris, Peter Ritchie, Lord Rowallan, Ian White, along with the archivists of the *Daily Record*, the Bank of Scotland and the Clydesdale Bank. Special thanks go to Maud Devine of East Renfrewshire Heritage Centre, for unfailing interest and professional assistance, and to all at Stenlake Publishing. A number of photographs featured in the book and dating from the 1890–1920 period were taken by W. O. Lindsay. The originals are now in the keeping of D. W. Blair. We acknowledge the late Inspector Hyslop of Giffnock police station and Mrs Hyslop, and also the late Alexander Cunningham, who in turn preserved and passed on Mr Lindsay's pictures.

The publishers would like to thank Robert Grieves for providing the picture on the front cover; Alistair Anderson for the picture on the back cover; and East Renfrewshire Council for the pictures on the following pages: 12, 13, 17 (right), 24, 25, 26 (both), 29, 33, 34, 38, 40 (both) and 41.

FURTHER READING

The books listed below were used by the author during her research. None of them is available from Stenlake Publishing. Those interested in finding out more are advised to contact their local bookshop or reference library.

Eastwood District, History and Heritage, Thomas C. Welsh
Sandstone to Suburbia, Eastwood District Library Team
The Kirk on the Hill, A. Blair
The History of the Montgomeries of Eglinton, Galston Library
Long Slope, Small Hill, D. Blair
Old Eastwood, Giffnock, Clarkston and Thornliebank, Ian L. Cormack
Old Newton Mearns, Anne Loudon and David Kidd

AUTHOR'S NOTE

The words 'currently' etc. used in the text refer to the status quo in the year 2003. The road through the centre of Giffnock has been known at different times as the Main Road, Kilmarnock Road and (currently) Fenwick Road. It is referred to in the text according to the date of the relevant photograph. Although originally called Main Road, this was not the original route to Kilmarnock. The old Mearns Road from Clarkston, and the Pollokshaws / Stewarton / Kilmarnock road are older.

INTRODUCTION

GIFFNOCK: A hamlet in Eastwood Parish, Renfrewshire, 1¼ miles south of Pollokshaws. It has a station on the Glasgow and Busby Railway and lies near the extensive quarries of excellent building sandstone, called 'liver rock'. (*Ordnance Gazetteer of Scotland*, 1883)

The entry from the *Ordnance Gazetteer* of 1883 gives a quaint picture of a small settlement with a little rural industry, but the history of Giffnock as a named place with features still recognisable today tails far back into the Middle Ages.

The name Gisnok (later spelled Gisnoc, Gifnok and Giffnock) appears to have been connected with the mention in 1265 of a household at Corslie Castle, a keep of some kind believed to have stood on the woodland rise near the present site of Woodfarm School. Religious oversight of the castle community would have been by the monks of Paisley Abbey. The position of the keep (among trees five or six miles east of Paisley) surely gave rise to the name 'Eastwood'. 'Corslie' itself brings us 'Crosslees', a name still prominent in the Spiersbridge area. The castle, its inhabitants and the surrounding buildings and their occupants would have formed a small community with a ruling family as tenants of a greater landowner. In the community there would have been gatemen, kitchen skivvies, goatherds, milkmaids, growers of kale and herb-crop, hunters finding food on the moorland, and women who cooked and served or drew water from burns. Some would have done several tasks.

265 years later, in 1530, comes documented reference to another landmark – Rockend (Ruken) Mill – noted when James V presented the surrounding land to the Montgomerie Earl of Eglinton of the time, already a considerable landowner in south-west Scotland. The Eglinton connection persists to the present day in a number of Giffnock street names including Winton Avenue, Egidia Avenue, Otterburn Drive, and Montgomery [*sic*] Drive.

Named on Blaeu's map of 1654 were scatterings of hamlets and crofting strips in an area labelled 'Gisnok part of Clydesdail'. The area was fertile, watered by criss-crossing burns, and by the 1750s the rigs or lanes of crops were giving way to hedged and ditched fields forming enclosed areas farmed by tenants whose homes sat within their own rented acreages. Lord Eglinton was one of half a dozen so-called 'improving' Scottish landowners who pioneered the changes, and by the 1780s there were nine or ten such farms around Giffnock, including Orchard, Gifnok, Braidbar, Mains, Henry's Croft, Davieland, Crosslees, Bagabout and Birkenshaw.

Before long several 'big houses' had been built around the edges of the farmland, including Birkenshaw in the Ruken area and Eastwood House, established in its own park *c*.1820 by Thomas Graham, lawyer and merchant. Later owners of Eastwood House were Thomas Smith and Joseph Wakefield. There was also Eastwoodhill, built for a Netherlee mill-owner, William Miller, in 1852, and Redhurst House, constructed *c*.1895 for the brick and tile manufacturer Mr Yuille who built the still familiar red railway bridges spanning Eastwoodmains Road. But these large houses and farms still lay scattered across the moorland with only rutted roadways connecting them to one another and similar landmarks.

In addition to agriculture there was another layer to what was now firmly 'Giffnock' on the map, with considerable local industry evident by the early to mid-nineteenth century. One activity was the extracting of limestone from a lime-pit by the burn alongside where Florence Drive now runs. Buggies of lime were led uphill to the later site of Orchardhill Church where the material was processed for building use. There was also the working of a coal seam in the Burnfield hollow. The coal was more suitable for industrial than household use, with customers including the Busby Gas Company which was supplying street lighting locally by this time. However, most important of the industries were the quarries along the north border of Giffnock in the Burnfield area, past the police-station site, and up the old Braidbar Farm road, from where high quality sandstone was extracted.

Until the 1860s almost all the glimpses into Giffnock's history, covering a period of some 600 years, come from dates and documents. But by the mid-nineteenth century far-seeing men, newfangled with cameras, were active in the square mile that was called Giffnock, recording life in photographs for the fascination of those who came after them.

The modern village-suburb began with the laying of a railway line in 1864 from Bridge Street station to Busby and beyond. The sparse population of Giffnock merited no more than a 'halt', which was principally for passengers travelling to Newton Mearns and continuing their journey south by horse-bus. Then city families began to make excursions for picnics and rambles in the fields by the halt, and saw the possibility of settling there with a commuting train to let the men reach their Glasgow businesses. The halt soon became a station proper, and neat, roomy, stone cottages began to rise around it.

About a mile to the south at the old toll-crossroads (situated where the

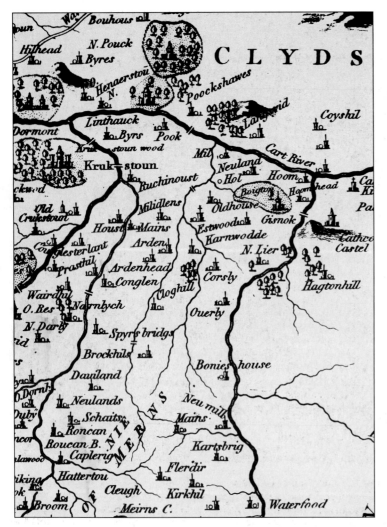

routes from Paisley to Busby and Glasgow to Newton Mearns crossed) other, grander houses were going up to accommodate wealthy merchants and the manager-rank from Mr Crum's printworks in Thornliebank. So then there were two clusters of newer houses alongside older farm cottages dotted among the fields. These new homes fronted the rough road running from Glasgow to the south and comprised the Giffnock of around 1890.

A need for recreation brought golf and bowling clubs, cycling and rambling groups. The desire for a local place of worship saw Giffnock Church established in 1900 on the hill above the Main Road, setting the seal of a true community on the village. Giffnock also needed more than the little Dame School that existed at the start of the twentieth century, and for eight or nine years a council primary school was sited in two rooms in the square tower of the church before a purpose-built school was raised on what became Academy Road. Shops, a local hall and flats followed in the red sandstone Maverton Building.

Gradually the farms disappeared under a rash of post-First World War housing. 1915 saw the construction of the police station and courthouse, and the old toll went through various incarnations as its crossroads was widened and realigned. Both Rouken Glen Park and the mansion houses with their extensive grounds had their own changing histories. A tragic new focal point appeared at the corner below Giffnock's second church at the toll. This was the memorial to 21 young men killed in the First World War, which had opened the quiet village to the world and unravelled the tight-knit community a little. Local industries had joined in the General Strike of 1926 and never recovered.

A thirties housing boom widened the area and made it denser both in population and bricks and mortar. The roads grew busier with cars, buses and lorries, and the cinema arrived. Royal events and the Second World War affected Giffnock as they did other places, and a number of pictures record what was peculiar to local experience and seen then as worth recording.

The original focal points of 150 years ago – the toll and station – are still there to symbolise the changes that have taken place over that time. But Nellie Niven, the erstwhile toll-keeper, would have to search for the crossroads that her cottage once stood next to, while at the station few of the passengers catching one of the half-hourly trains of 2003 to the city remember now that the halt there was what brought Giffnock its first settlers. Like other places it has been further enriched in the past 30 years with incomers from across the world, now good neighbours and welcome friends. 'Time', it is said, 'is what stops everything happening at once'. Historians should be thankful.

This map from Blaeu's atlas of 1654 provides a fascinating presentation of the relative positions of familiar farms, houses, rivers, woodland and castles, accompanied by just-recognisable spellings. The map was probably drafted by estimated measurement of distances between landmarks, by exploring local knowledge, by following burns and rivers and by much patient plodding about the countryside.

Rouken Glen House had a number of different names during its existence, being renamed Birkenshaw House then Thornliebank House. The surrounding parkland (originally Ruken lands) was called Birkenshaw Estate when it was bought from a Glasgow merchant by Walter Crum, master of Thornliebank printworks, in 1858. Birkenshaw Cottage stood nearby. The mansion house deserves mention for two nineteenth century visitors. One was Lord Kelvin, who as William Thomson spent time there partly meditating on a solution to the scientific problem of how to lay a sub-Atlantic cable (the feat which later brought him his peerage), and

The Mansion House, Rouken Glen.

partly in courting Margaret Crum, his future wife. A visitor remembered later with rather more of a frisson was Madeleine Smith, a regular summer guest at Birkenshaw with her family. She was tried in 1857 for the poisoning of her lover Emil L'Angelier. The jury's verdict was 'not proven', but the public was not so kind. A later Crum, nephew to Walter, let the estate for some years to Cameron Corbett MP, afterwards Lord Rowallan. He subsequently purchased the ivy-clad baronial mansion house with its crow-stepped gables, deep-arched porches and extensive grounds, to make a gift of them in 1906 to the people of Glasgow as a stately home and public park. For 40 years the house was a favourite afternoon-tea haunt, but was demolished shortly after the Second World War having suffered serious damage from its occupation by troops. Part of the stable block and the one-time head gardener's house, with their turn-of-the-century period features, are now used as a restaurant.

The easily extracted honey-coloured sandstone for which the area was famous lay alongside the north-eastern corner of Giffnock. During the 100 years of their working from 1830, when the Earl of Eglinton sold the land to developers of the industry, the Giffnock quarries produced huge quantities of stone. Material was provided for much of Victorian Glasgow, including the handsome architecture of Alexander 'Greek' Thomson. It also went into the City Chambers and parts of the university, and was used in the building of the parliamentary and government complexes in Australia, South Africa and Ireland. 1,000 men from Glasgow's Southside, working from 4 a.m. to 4 p.m., earned two shillings per day during much of that quarrying century. There were four quarries, three of which were worked from the surface and one from underground. This picture shows cliffs of stone with mazes of tunnels cut into the faces (the network of borings connected the quarries with each other). Visible too are the tracks for trucks carrying stone away from the workings. In early years the material went to nearby storage yards for onward transport by road, but by 1864 it was being trucked to the main railway line.

The view looking westward from what later became the site of Penrith and Eastwood Avenues c.1892. The railway line lies in the foreground, as it does today, with the end of the station platform to the right. At the right-hand edge of the picture is the stationmaster's cottage. Beyond the railway line is the land which became the site of Giffnock Primary School and Academy Road, while the cottage in the right-hand corner of that field served as the premises of the Clydesdale Bank from 1910 and marks the site of the bank's current premises. In front of the field runs the thoroughfare which for many years was called simply the Main Road. The house with the dormer windows facing it was first a private residence, then a dental practice, as it remains to date. Orchard Drive (then called Studio Road after a photographic studio in one of the houses on the right) runs towards the hill in the background, while the house on the right-hand corner, once a family home, is now the Royal Bank of Scotland. The wide slope in the background was first moorland, then a farm field and later Eastwood golf course, before being developed as Orchard Park housing estate from the mid-1930s. Barrland Drive, Dalmeny Avenue and the Kwik-Fit car repair business now lie across the Main Road from the stationmaster's cottage.

A country railway 'halt', grown up to become a real village station, was soon seen to need a stationmaster to oversee the comings and goings of the horse-carriages, pony traps and horse-bus, all of which connected daily with the trains. This solid, no-nonsense cottage appeared in 1870 in the station yard near the present-day public library, remaining a landmark for over 100 years. Behind it, in those pre-motor vehicle days, was stabling for the horse-bus animals. Besides the management of the station premises and the organising of personnel, passengers and freight, the stationmaster had duties on the industrial line laid between the main line and what became May Terrace. Buggies carrying industrial material away from the collieries, quarry and lime-pit ran on that track. The last stationmaster to inhabit the house was Andrew Goldie who lived there with his family until the 1960s. This picture dates from about 1959. The south gable of the Fenwick Road tenements can be seen on the right. The cottage, like the several coal merchants' offices in the station yard, was demolished to make way for the library when it was moved in 1982 from Rhuallan House, and to lay out an extensive car park.

There had been coal-mining in Giffnock since 1850, the pits being entered from the area between the railway line and Burnfield Road. Mining was first carried out by Alexander Frame and later by Messrs Barr & Thornton who sank deeper shafts. Later the mineral rights passed to Giffnock Collieries. At their peak 300 miners were employed at the Giffnock pits, coming to work there from various Southside village communities. Workings in the coal seams underground spidered out to what are now Hillpark and Merrylee, and as far as Eastwood Toll. It was said that people walking above ground at some points could hear the singing of the miners far below, and mining continued until the General Strike of 1926. Over in the station yard there were several coal merchants' offices built like small cottages. Kennedy's was established in 1877. Here householders could order and pay for quality coal and coal products such as briquettes and ovoids. These companies did not sell the Burnfield coal as it was of relatively poor quality, more suitable for small industries such as those in Thornliebank and Pollokshaws than household use, and the coal supplied from the station yard came from further afield in Lanarkshire. Between Kennedy's and May Terrace (the roofs of the houses of which can be seen in the background) were the main railway line and the small industrial buggy line which ran alongside it.

Eastwood Park lodge and entrance gates differ little now from their appearance in the 1920s. However, when this picture was taken the small, nineteenth century baronial-style house seemed to be much further down Rouken Glen Road, as Eastwood Toll was then situated 100 yards to the east. Various high-profile visitors came through this gate to see Lord and Lady Weir during the period they lived at Eastwood House. King George V and Queen Mary visited and on such occasions the royal train was parked at Whitecraigs station. Stanley Baldwin and General Smuts, Laurel and Hardy and Sir Harry Lauder were other guests and during the weeks leading up to the abdication of 1936, Edward VIII was seen being driven in at this entrance. The imposing black and gold triple main gate with its six pillars was presented to Viscount Weir soon after 1945 in recognition of his contribution to the Second World War effort and is now the principal entrance. This photograph was taken from the entrance gate to The Hollows, the large house opposite the lodge. For many years this was occupied by the Sawers family, owners of a chain of high-class Glasgow fishmongers. It sat on the site of recently-built luxury flats (1999) at the start of the road to Newton Mearns, on its west side.

About a mile south of Giffnock station was the crossing of the roads from Paisley to Busby and Glasgow to Newton Mearns. The narrow road to the left (later Eastwoodmains Road) led to Busby, Eaglesham and East Kilbride, while that to the right led to Spiersbridge. The road straight ahead continued through countryside to Newton Mearns, then over the Fenwick Moor to Kilmarnock. Nowadays the road layout has changed greatly at this point, with the old Kilmarnock Road running past the stone bank building (seen on page 31 and presently a restaurant) and the front entrance to the now-demolished Macdonald Hotel, before dividing in two, with a wide loop passing round the Mains Estate and a spur petering out into a cul-de-sac and narrow, overgrown footpath curving out on to the Ayr Road again. A realignment re-routes the Newton Mearns road (as Ayr Road) by means of a wide roundabout a hundred yards to the west of the original tollhouse. When this photograph was taken in the late 1880s, the crossroads was a gathering place for so many milk carts that the Newton Mearns road was known as the 'Milky Way'. Tolls were collected at the white cottage by a lady called Nellie Niven and the corner was, for many years, called Nellie's Toll. Typical toll charges at one period ranged from sixpence for carts, to three shillings for a gentleman's six-horse carriage, a penny for an ox, ass or head of cattle to free passage for a dog-cart or builder's barrow.

This picture looks eastward along the 'made' but rough country road running from Spiersbridge to Nellie's Toll shortly before 1900. Those were still days when the track-like road would have had only cart, pony-trap, milk-float or carriage traffic. Note the clumps of grass on the verges and the rough, broken kerb. The wall on the right marked the boundary of Rouken Glen Estate, and the cottage was one of the houses built around the park for senior estate workers. These and the entrance on the right are still part of the scene, as is the woodland round them. On the left is what is still the lower (west) part of Eastwood Park grounds. The tramline from Glasgow, with its red-painted cars, reached Eastwood Toll in 1905 and within a year – during which Rouken Glen had become a Mecca for weekend outings for Glaswegians – the track was extended west to the park gates. At this point it met the tram route from Thornliebank, forming a complete loop to and from the city. The old road in the photograph was then upgraded and became Eastwoodmains Road West.

Mains Farmhouse, sitting in the midst of a 1940s/50s development of luxury villas, is reckoned to be the oldest surviving house in Giffnock, built in 1763 on an area of ancient farmland. By the first half of the 1800s a second house, Mains House, stood nearby in the same huge grounds called the Mains Estate. An entrance to Mains Estate stood across the road from the former Macdonald Hotel, with stone-pillared gates opening onto the driveway to farm and house and one or two farm cottages. Mains House, a two-storey Georgian-style dwelling-house, was the childhood home of Gordon Davidson (now of Mearns) and his sisters, their parents and paternal grandparents. He recalls that the family always referred to the farmhouse (which was the home of his maternal grandmother) as 'the Manor'. This view of the white-painted 'manor' or farmhouse at 6 Cadzow Avenue shows the rear of

the building, including some additions to the house that Don Davidson knew. Its real front faces away from the road. The stone Mains House with its large conservatory was demolished c.1973 and the old glory is only now remembered by the worn gate-pillars, which were removed from the entrance to the estate, brought up the hill and placed at the driveway into the complex of fine flats which took the house's place in 1974. An elderly lady with a wide knowledge of Giffnock remembers it being said that a small room in the Manor was kept for the use of John Galt (1779–1839), Ayrshire-born poet and author of the novel *The Annals of the Parish*, so that he could spend time writing there.

Until it was demolished in the late 1950s, Redhurst was one of the oldest houses in Giffnock. It sat, quirky as a dolls' house with its shiny tiles, oriels and roof peaks, set back from the corner of Eastwoodmains Road and Broomley Lane. Some early form of the building seems to have existed on the site c.1861, first as a tied house on farmland, then as a private residence. But the later house with its lodge (called Ingleneuk) dated from about 1895. It was owned by Mr and Mrs Yuille who ran the local brickworks. The company built the two red-brick rail bridges still to be seen spanning Eastwoodmains Road and Sutherland Drive. Redhurst was finally demolished to make way for a modern hotel of the same name, although somewhere inside the modern lodge-bungalow is the old tied cottage of Ingleneuk.

Until the 1890s Sundays saw the Giffnock settlers walking or travelling by pony trap to the churches they had attended before moving to the new village-suburb. A few began to meet in the station waiting room and later, more formally, in the clubhouse of Eastwood Golf Club at the end of what is now Orchard Drive, beside the site of Abbeyfield House. Oil lanterns lit their way on winter evenings and hymns were accompanied by an American 'wheelie' organ. As the community outgrew these makeshift arrangements, plans were drawn up for a proper parish church. Among the leading lights in overseeing plans for the church – built on the hill halfway between the station and the tollhouse – were the pioneering worthies William Mann and William Johnstone. The first service was held on 13 May 1900, and by the end of the day the cost of £3,000 had been fully met and the congregation was free of debt. Having opened as a 'preaching station' the church soon became part of the United Free Church of Scotland. The transepts and hall were not built until later.

This photograph was taken *c*.1877 at the village sports day and garden party. The event was held in a field among farm buildings and included a competition for the best-dressed young lady and her bicycle . . . and maybe the most magnificent hat. The scene suggests a more leisured (but surely industrious age), when television and computer games were unheard of!

About 1890 the 'muir' at the end of the lane that became Orchard Drive was acquired and a golf course of nine holes was laid out on it. This picture shows the course's opening day in 1891, the view facing west across fields and farmland to the ridge separating Giffnock and Thornliebank. The whole area is now the Giffnock side of Orchard Park Estate, but at the time the players shared their rural course with sheep and cattle. Considering that this was still a relatively new area, the picture shows a large gathering with well over 50 people present. Eastwood Golf Club took off, marking another step on the way to suburban Giffnock. But there was a snag. Local tradition tells that an existing stone cottage situated near the first tee had begun to be used as a makeshift clubhouse. But when it was found that quarry explosives were stored there a large number of cautious members resigned. They found land near Pollokshaws and formed Pollok Golf Club there. Some time later, back at the Giffnock muir, the Eastwood course was re-established and a purpose-built red-roofed clubhouse raised on the site of the present Abbeyfield House. It remained a well-used hall long after the club's definitive move in the 1930s out to the Fenwick Moor.

Hoopla day at the bowling club! Bowling was one of the earliest recreations to be taken up with enthusiasm as Giffnock gradually turned itself into a true community and, since opening between Percy Drive and Redhurst House in 1895, the club has flourished and expanded. Fund-raising has always been a feature of club life, partly for the social pleasure it has brought and partly, as everywhere, to keep its treasurers happy. The hat and suit of the gentleman on the right with his quoit, and the girl's school hat and dark socks, suggest that this picture must have been taken at a club fete in the late 1920s or early 1930s.

16

By the late 1920s and early 1930s rambling was a popular pursuit all over Scotland. The cheerful Giffnock group in this photograph has reached the ruins of Crookston Castle on a hillside near Paisley Road (one of the many south Glasgow sites connected, by tradition, with Mary, Queen of Scots). The period of the picture is confirmed by the representative variety of headgear and clothing: 'doolander' caps (a doolander was a wide, flat 'bunnet' that resembled the platform on a pigeon loft!), soft hats and bowlers on the men; cloche hats and fur tippets on the ladies.

Occasionally a simple community produces a kind of Renaissance man or woman, multi-talented and generous with his or her gifts. Alec Turnbull was one of these, a pawky but gentle, self-effacing man who had an ancestry and aura that might have the makings of a character in a novel. The opening chapters would relate that both his father and grandfather were seagoing – captains of sailing-ships – and both were lost at sea. Alec himself was born in 1909 in Grangemouth and came to Giffnock as a young boy. This *c.*1928 photograph of him was taken in the days of the Boys' Brigade pillbox, rifle and highly polished shoes. It portends a lifelong commitment to the BB, most of it as captain of the 254th Glasgow Company at Giffnock South Parish Church. Although there is more than one BB company flourishing in Giffnock in 2003, the 254th has been a bastion of the movement for over 70 years, and seen armies of boys through its ranks. This single laddie symbolises them all. Following father and grandfather, Alec spent his working life with a shipping company, the Donaldson Line, but as a landlubber, not at sea. Nor did war take him sailing. He served out the years of the Second World War in the Royal Artillery. When that period was over he joined with a group of musical friends to form a concert party as one of its pianists, singer, rhymester, poet and raconteur. For 50 years they have performed for charity, entertaining groups in homes and clubs and for sheer love of word and music. In his retirement Alec moved to Eastwoodhill House, some 300 yards from the home where he had lived with his wife, Nan. Even there he found a niche as ballad-maker, minstrel and general artistic asset. Alec died aged 94 in 2003.

Throughout the early days of Giffnock the same names recur over and over in different areas of initiative – kirk matters, golf, bowling, council business and Scouting – suggesting a busy core of community-minded individuals, both men and women. Prominent names include the Johnstones, Kyles, Mitchells, Thomsons, Manns and others. Even before the Giffnock Scouts were officially founded in 1912, there were one or two patrols scouting away, eager but unattached. With the support of a few local gentlemen they set up as the 28th Glasgow (Giffnock) Scout Group, meeting first at the 'tin academy'. When the school was demolished in 1912 (for the stone one to take its place) a Scout hall costing £53 was raised first on the site of the police station, then taken down and re-erected the same year at the opening of Braidbar Farm lane, beside Robertsons' riding school and the old Giffnock forge (the site now near the start of Braidpark Drive). During the First World War, when Scoutmasters were away, patrol leaders kept the group going. This photograph shows the 28th drawn up outside that original hut, ready to leave it in 1936 for the sturdy new brick and pebbled hall in Arthurlie Drive, built following enthusiastic fund-raising and a very generous donation.

This picture shows the opening ceremony in 1936 of the new hall in Arthurlie Drive and includes local ministers E. O. Rodger and H. C. MacKenzie, Guide leaders and Scouters with long-time group Scoutmaster Joe Kyle to the left of the door. It is a small irony that Rudolf Hess, who landed five years later in 1941 at Eaglesham and was brought on that occasion to this hall, was actually trying to find the man at the centre of this picture – the future Duke of Hamilton – who as local MP performed the opening ceremony. Hess was five years too late! For nearly 70 years the hall has seen generations of Cubs and Scouts meeting here week by week, and the building has become a well-loved social asset for Giffnock folk.

A group of Giffnock parents and Scouts at camp at Catacol, Arran, in 1932.

Orchard House (now Orchard Park Hotel) was built in the midst of what had been Orchard Farm, the most extensive farmland and heart of the Giffnock area. Before the name Giffnock or any of its other spellings was on maps at all, the locality was marked on charts as 'Orchard'. This solid, grey villa, domed, balconied and with interesting roof features, was built around the start of last century close to where the farmhouse had been. The original gate sat diagonally across the corner of Park and Main Roads and the blocked-off remains of it can still be seen. The house itself has a handsome entrance, richly carved stonework and is lit by many large windows. In its early days (when Park Road was still a rough cul-de-sac) it was occupied by the owner of Orchard Farm, and then by other private residents. Subsequently it became a maternity nursing home for the baby boom of the 1950s, and then the popular hotel and restaurant of modern times. Inside, many of the house's original features are still to be seen in its stained glass, mouldings and woodwork.

One of the more kenspeckle examples of Giffnock architecture is the Maverton Building on Fenwick Road, sitting about halfway between the police station and Eastwood Toll. The complex is on a slight ridge sloping down towards the rear at Maryville Avenue. Originally, in the very early twentieth century, there was only a hall on the site, below road level at the front and entered from the back. This was the social hub of the village, the venue for chamber concerts, dances, political meetings and film shows featuring comedies and early newsreels (one was of the cross-channel flight of Louis Bleriot). The embryonic congregation of Giffnock South Church met there between 1912 and 1914 before settling at Eastwood Toll, first in halls and in 1929 in the present handsome stone church. Some years after the opening of the Maverton hall, a row of shops was built above it, with four well-built flats over them, unusually for Giffnock in red sandstone. The rich stonework, finials and arched windows, along with two pillared entrances and stained glass, still remain features. In due course the hall below was divided into shop basements and the only evidence visible of it now are pillars inside supporting the overbuilding.

Tom, Alexander and Frank Law sit engrossed in a game of draughts. Frank (right), the youngest of this trio of brothers, was an early settler in Giffnock and lived most of his life in the area. The photograph was taken by his father in 1897. As well as being a study in concentration of players and spectator, the group and setting provide an interesting social picture of the period. It shows what small boys wore or, noting the bare feet, did not wear when relaxing at home: the broad galluses (braces) and the collarless shirts. When worn at school or church, these shirts would have taken the wide Eton-type collars (often made of washable celluloid) which were the fashion of the time. A century later, in 2003, the boys' cut-to-the-knuckle hairstyle has come round full-circle. The adjustable stool under the draught board indicates that there was a piano in the house, as in many middle-class homes of the time.

A photograph like this – showing the maid with one of the children – could have been taken in almost any garden in the Giffnock of the years up to the Second World War. By 1945 general housemaids were a departed species, but here, c.1917, Lizzie Martin is to be seen in her morning uniform of cap, wrapper-dress and long apron. (Afternoon wear would have been black and white with stiff cuffs, lace collar and cap). Lizzie is remembered as having been as firm with the family in the parlour as in her kitchen. She is seen here with Miss Nan Gardner, aged about three. Miss Gardner is aptly named for having had one of the finest and most interesting gardens in Eastwood – double-feued, and long-retaining Victorian touches. She is equally known as a fine musician and needlewoman.

Nan Gardner has lived almost her whole life within little more than a hundred yards of the spot where this photograph and the one opposite were taken. The garden she is seen in on the facing page was that of first her grandparents, then her parents, then of Miss Gardner herself. The house was called 'Ellerslie' and along with the adjoining semi-villa was one of the earliest Giffnock homes. It is also one of the most charming, situated off Orchard Drive and built *c*.1892. The architectural style is unusual. It is plain and elegant in light grey sandstone with classical proportions and, as the picture shows, with the casement or sash side-curtains of the period. The interior features fine woodwork, fireplaces, stained glass and an unusual tessellated entrance hallway.

KILMARNOCK ROAD, GIFFNOCK.

This early twentieth century picture shows the stretch of Kilmarnock Road running through Giffnock between Park Road (in the distance) and Station Road, which curves past the tree and shop to lead into what is now the station car park. In those days the main road presented a very different picture from that of 2003, although the villas on the left (east) side are still a feature of the view. The road itself was narrow, not yet having undergone either of its two widenings. Between the gable of the first semi-villa on the left and the cottage runs the short Orchard Park. On the right, the turn of the pavement into Orchard Drive can be seen beyond what is now the Royal Bank of Scotland (hidden by foliage). During the slump of the 1920s men who had been unemployed were brought in to widen the road, a process which necessitated the shortening of the gardens lining it. There was a second widening 50 years later. In the picture ploughing towards the camera is a tramcar, very properly on the left-hand track, while the nearer horse and cart appears to have a more casual attitude to the rule of the road, trotting along on the right. It would have been into this road from the near left corner of the picture that the station horse-bus turned on its way to Mearns.

This view of Kilmarnock Road was taken later than the one opposite (as can be seen from the growth of the tree in the foreground) but also predates the first road-widening of *c*.1926. I recall going with my father in the 1930s into the cottage across the road from the villa gable when this housed the Clydesdale Bank. The property had been bought by the bank in 1910, and was demolished in the late 1930s when the present red sandstone Clydesdale Bank building was constructed on the site, with accommodation adjoining it for the manager and his family. From the late 1920s/early 30s the shop in the foreground was a newsagent's and post office run by Harry Sheppard. Alfred Fletcher later expanded the premises and business which remained there until the 1990s, at one stage alongside a small ironmonger's. In 2003 the site is occupied by another newsagent and post office and Andiamo's restaurant.

Giffnock School.

Giffnock Primary School, *c*.1935. By the start of the twentieth century, Giffnock required more than Miss Gardner's little Dame School at Ingleneuk, the lodge of Redhurst, and a council school was opened in the tower of the new Giffnock Church. It in turn was vacated for the 'tin academy', a corrugated iron shed with two classrooms on a site between the railway line (alongside what is now Penrith Avenue) and Kilmarnock Road. By 1911 the purpose-built stone building in the picture had been opened as Giffnock Primary School. That was the Coronation year of George V and a crest of that date, surmounted by a crown, was carved into the north outside wall (now within a new extension). The school had eight teachers and 250 pupils. This photograph was taken about 25 years later, when hut classrooms had been added. The boys outside the playground are in typical summer clothing of the time. The current playground railings are new, but the rusted stubs of the original ones are evidence of the removal of all iron railings to make munitions in World War II.

The person who turned the lens on this scene must have stood somewhere between what later became the sites of Wellfield Avenue and Park Church, perhaps on the old Eastwood golf course. Whatever its precise position, the camera, facing east, has recorded a field of corn stooks in what must have been one of the last pieces of farmland in the Giffnock village area, productive until the 1920s. In the background is the block of twelve tenement flats on what is now called Fenwick Road, with the four houses of Knowe Terrace adjoining it. Within ten years of the photograph being taken almost 60 houses forming Barrland Drive and Dalmeny Avenue, with a row of ten shops opposite the tenements, lay on the cornfield. By the next decade the Tudor Cinema had been built on what is the extreme left of the view. The field would have been part of Orchard Farm, which in its heyday stretched almost from Nellie's Toll to the Burnfield Road area, the most extensive of all the ancient farms.

This Infant 3 class photograph was taken at Giffnock Primary School *c*.1934/35, nearly a quarter of a century after the sandstone school opened in 1911. It is interesting to see a sprinkling of children, among those in the ordinary clothes of the time, wearing the school uniform that would become usual a few years later. In the middle background are the rear of the semi-villas at Nos. 239 and 241 of what is now Fenwick Road. As far as fallible memory serves (and with apologies for errors and omissions) these are the children's names. The teacher was Miss Ballantine.

Back row: Donald Anderson; _____; Billy Ross; Jim Miller; Bill Martin; George Ireland; Malcolm ___; Douglas Ronald; Peter Turnbull.

Third row: _____; Ian White; Ian Lane/Laing; Ronald Milne; _____; Willie Gemmell; Sandy ___; Norval Wallace; Campbell Grant; Dorothy Pearce; June McEwan

Second row: Jean Wilson; Doreen Raine; Margaret Smith; Mary Dawson; Mary Huddleston; ___ McCulloch; Doreen McAlister; Margaret Wyllie; Margaret Beck; May Spottiswood; Muriel Benjamin; Sheila Wilson

Front row: Nancy McKay; Pamela Beith; Anna Law; Joyce Pollock; Sheila Kilgour; ___ Cumming; Maisie Gill; Betty Peddie

Situated beyond the bowling green, the imposing grey houses of Broomley Drive were, in the early twentieth century, on the still-rural eastern edge of Giffnock, facing up towards Clarkston and the old village of Busby. The houses overlooked extensive farmland which stretched up to the Glasgow/Busby railway line and beyond. Within the picture on the right the railway bridge spanning Eastwoodmains Road can be seen. Behind the rear gardens of the houses ran the little Broomley burn (as it still does). These photographs were taken from an upstairs window in the Broomley Drive home of the Gardner family. Later, instead of looking out over the farm fields and buildings, another photographer would have seen single-storey houses on the other side of the drive, where the fence and row of posts are here. At a still later date the view beyond that would have been of Williamwood Golf Course. By about 1938 the golf course area was covered by fine bungalows in Lawrence, Ruthven, Deveron, Balvie and Melford Avenues, and Sutherland, Kensington, Evan, Brora, Clyth and Etive Drives.

When the photographer looked out from his window in Broomley Drive early last century over farm fields and later Williamwood Golf Course, he could not have visualised that by the late 1930s the area would be covered by neat, well-built bungalows which are now more desirable than ever. Owners, reluctant to leave them for larger homes, have instead found great scope for extending them. Those in the picture lie in Sutherland Drive, Lawrence and Ruthven Avenues, and a network of other wide roads between Broomley burn, with its little footbridge, and the railway line seen here as a ridge on the skyline. Also visible is one of the two Yuille brick bridges spanning Eastwoodmains Road. The whole Williamwood area was developed by John Lawrence (also of Rangers football fame) and is bordered by the burn, Eastwoodmains Road and the curve of the railway line from Giffnock station to the red bridges.

This is one of the later views of Eastwood Toll, with a row of shops – comprising James Davie's grocery, a chemists, R. S. McColl's and A. F. Reid's bakery and tea shop – having taken the place of Nellie Niven's cottage. The style of the gas lamps and the type of tram (about to sweep round into what became Rouken Glen Road) dates the picture as being from the later 1920s or early 1930s. All that Nellie would have recognised of her rural corner of 40 years before would have been the sturdy tree growing at the gable of the baker's shop (the same tree is seen in its young and spindly days on page 10). In the centre of the picture, above the shops, is the roof and part of the gable of a house which was once the home of a Crum manager, later the district council offices and then successively a local clinic, BUPA centre, and now the premises of the Elphinstone Group, a firm of property developers. The calm and classic interior furnishing of its current occupants probably reflects the period in which this gracious house was built better than any of its other recent incarnations.

By the time this 1930s picture was taken Nellie Niven's tollhouse was long gone, having been demolished in 1910 and replaced by this row of shops. The neatly kerbed, well-surfaced road with its tramlines swinging round towards Rouken Glen reveals the progress of Giffnock from country village to suburb that had been made by the 1930s. Glasgow Corporation's tram service from Newlands to Eastwood Toll commenced on 17 June 1905. Routes at that time were allocated colours displayed as a broad band round the upper deck. The Millerston/Giffnock tram was the 'red car'. Eventually proliferation of routes called for numbering instead of identification by colours, and in May 1938 the red route became No. 8. The service was withdrawn in March 1959 in favour of No. 38 buses which also ran to Rouken Glen.

The changing face of Eastwood Toll is seen here, with the road having been upgraded from the original rough track to this paved surface with cobbled tram lane. On the hill to the left is the second Giffnock church, Giffnock South Parish Church, built in 1929 for an already existing congregation. The war memorial in the curve of the hedge was erected shortly after the church. On the corner to the right is the handsome triangular stone Bank of Scotland building with crow-stepping and a sturdy balustrade at roof level above the front elevation. The rear of the building was rented to accommodate a main Giffnock post office. The building plans for the block, costed at £8,000, date from 1929 (the same year the new church went up), and the bank opened for business in 1931.

When Nellie Niven of the old tollhouse at the south end of Giffnock hung out her washing in her corner garden, with her back towards Glasgow, she would have looked straight ahead in the direction of Newton Mearns. To her right she would have seen the road to Spiersbridge. To her left there would have been the tree-lined avenue running towards Williamwood, Clarkston and Busby. But this photograph of Eastwoodmains Road was taken long after Nellie had pegged out her last petticoat. Although much is the same now, this view dates from the 1930s. The lady in the long skirt may seem to belong to an earlier period, but one can't argue with Belisha beacons! The road leading off to the right is Denholm Drive, and that to the left is Otterburn Drive, while the row of shops in the distance was built in the 1930s on what had been part of Williamwood Golf Course.

This picture was taken from the north edge of Giffnock over 60 years later than that on page 24 featuring horse and cart and tramcar. Prominent here are the oldest flats in Giffnock, which according to an early resident, Jack Greenshields, were built between 1910 and 1920. They were perhaps unlikely to have been constructed between 1914 and 1918, and so are probably pre-war or immediately post-war. The flats were known then (along with the adjacent row of four houses) as Knowe Terrace. They contain four apartments and are entered through handsome tiled ('wally') closes with rounded, arched landing windows in stained glass. Altogether they compare with the best Glasgow tenements of the art nouveau style. It was not until the late 1930s that the second block of flats, Wellfield Court, appeared in the district, this time in art deco style. It is evidence of changing patterns of domestic life that by the end of the twentieth century there were large and small flats in every gap among the villas, terraces and bungalows of earlier days, many of them occupied not by families but by single people, young and old.

It was the late 1990s. The pizza parlour was opening beside Safeway supermarket and having its shopfront constructed. Elderly passers-by were stopped in their tracks by the sight of a much-loved name revealed as the new sign went into place. Seventy years ago, standing alone opposite the Main Road tenement, was the ice-cream shop, Pelosi's Cafe. Within a few years in the 1930s a row of shops was built alongside it, and the cafe had become the rendezvous for Giffnock's young, with its long marble and cast-iron tables and shiny bench seats. There, hands were held, confidences exchanged, confessions made and tiffs blew up. MacCallum ice-creams were ordered (vanilla ice-cream with raspberry sauce), sly cigarettes were puffed . . . even homework was done. Everything in the cafe took place under the stern eyes of sister and brothers Annie, Jimmy and Louis Pelosi and their comely niece Mary. They looked out on the scene over their high sweetie counter and, one and all, could quell trouble with a glance. Youngsters were stunned when Pelosi's closed and a building society set up shop. Nowadays perhaps the pizza place is the new teenage haunt, but somehow it seems too grown-up, too fast-food-and-hurry-out. And there isn't a Pelosi in sight.

One of the notable early twentieth century inhabitants of Giffnock was Edith White, a lady of considerable artistic and creative gifts. For over 40 years from the early 1930s, generations of girls flocked to her dance classes, held at her home studio in St Anne's Drive and later at the larger venues needed for ever-increasing numbers of pupils. She was also a talented interior decorator and water-colourist . . . and a quirky, humorous personality to boot! A display by her dance classes was held annually in Marlborough House, Shawlands, or other reception halls. This group, showing the wide age-range of her students, are in Grecian pose.

Back row: Blanche Knox; Cochrane Kellock; Dorothy Hammond; Margaret Cameron; _____
Middle row: Betty Taylor; Audrey Young; Dorothy Andrew; Aileen Sharpe; _____; Jean Kellock; Winifred Sharpe
Front row: Kathleen Geyer; _____; _____; Fiona McCulloch; Anna Law; _____; Betty Peddie; _____; Dorothy McCall

Glasgow in the 1920s, 30s and 40s was known as Cinema City, with 90 picture-houses within the city boundaries. Many of these were on the south side of the river and in early days a varied cluster of them – from flea-pits to palaces – were located around Shawlands and Battlefield. These were much patronised by Giffnock people. Then in 1936 the Tudor Cinema appeared in its white stucco, art deco style of architecture with pink, blue and green neon lighting. It was situated on the site of the present Safeway supermarket and its then modern and flamboyant style aroused some small dissent from douce villagers. But this soon died away in the eagerness to see what was 'on'. The film shown in the opening week was, appropriately, *Tudor Rose*. The complex included wedding-reception rooms, ballroom, restaurant and small meeting-rooms. Integral to the building and facing on to Kilmarnock Road were several shops: Birrell's confectioner's (for your sweeties for the pictures), a ladies' outfitter, chemist, and optician. The Tudor became a real community centre and thrived throughout the Second War until television brought dwindling audiences. Nevertheless, it was much mourned when the sliding gates clanged shut for the last time in 1962.

This photograph shows the old Braidbar Nurseries site at the corner of a little-known, slightly mysterious lane, once the entrance to a small piggery and marked on old maps as Merrylee Park Lane. It is said that the broad Merrylee Park Avenue, developed almost opposite in the mid-1930s, was made extra wide to be a through-road with the lane. If widened, this would have led into the embryonic Burnfield Road, subsequently reaching Thornliebank. The Second World War apparently thwarted the plan to widen the lane, which may still be gathering dust somewhere, and it remained unaltered for many years with the landmark of a spacious bungalow at its opening. This was demolished *c*.2000. The lane has since been tidied up and surfaced for half of its length. A little way down among fir trees on the left nestles a fine mid-twentieth century house. On the right-hand side further down lies Carleton Gate housing complex, which has replaced the old nursery, long a popular feature of the area. The Braidbar was laid out with a tempting array of garden plants sold along with good horticultural advice to aspiring gardeners.

Babywear, bobbins and buttons, lades' underwear, pins and needles and wools of every colour and ply . . . Jean Noble's shop was a treasure store in Giffnock. It stood for many decades in the row of shops opposite the old tenement, and there wasn't much in the drapery line and gift business that couldn't be found there. The shop was run by Jean, Lily and Margaret Noble with cousins and friends on hand to help serve and exchange local news. These pictures of the shop's interior show Miss Lily Noble and another member of staff serving the constant flow of customers who enjoyed the 'crack' and social hubbub. There can have been few Giffnock women who were not regulars at Jean Noble's and there was a long collective sigh when the shop finally closed down in the 1990s.

A potted history of Giffnock vehicular traffic after the days of horse, cart and carriage would range over a hundred years. It would pass from the first remembered motorcar, the Arrol–Johnston of 1902 belonging to Robert Anderson of Eastwoodhill, which cruised through Giffnock to the delight of small boys and the envy of grown men; through the days, shortly afterwards, when there was a 10 mph speed limit along the Main Road; and on to the modern stream of cars, buses and vans that course through the suburb now. Included in that history would be the plethora of service-stations/garages that have come and gone over a century. There were pumps and mechanics at Eastwood Toll, as well as Burns & Fulton's garage on the site of the modern Kwik-Fit premises, and the business illustrated here called the Braidbar Motor Company, which sat near the Congregational (now United Reformed) Church. Close to its site was what was known as the 'bottomless quarry' which claimed more than one life before it was fenced off. That it was not bottomless was proved by its eventual infilling for the outdoor area of the Fairbairn car sales complex.

Although slightly outwith what is thought of as the 'Giffnock mile', and oddly named for its situation, Orchard Park filling station did sit beside the old Giffnock Farm (demolished in the 1990s). It was located opposite the opening to Merrycrest Avenue and was another of the service points for increasing traffic through Giffnock and from the city. The photograph dates from c.1975.

The celebrations for the Silver Jubilee of King George V in 1935 included the laying out of a commemorative playing field on land at the foot of Huntly Avenue. An almost indecipherable plaque is still to be found at the side of the entrance-gate confirming this. Almost at once this became a hugely popular sports venue and still remains so. It was much-used during the Second World War for fund-raising rallies and fetes, personality appearances and the rousing of patriotic fervour. This photograph was taken at a 1941 wartime fete and shows a march past featuring the nursing section of the blanket Civil Defence organisation. The nursing caps were still of the flowing kind, and, here and there, are CDV (Civil Defence Volunteer) and ARP (Air Raid Precaution (Service)) tin hats. Taking the salute was the local MP Sir Guy Lloyd. The roofs to the right are those of the then new houses at the lower end of Forres Avenue. Beyond Forres Avenue, alongside the playing field, lay part of the water-filled Giffnock/Muirend quarry complex, deep and dangerous. Eventually this was filled in and the park was extended into that area during the 1990s. Almost hidden in the woodland at the far end of the original pitches is a tiny Wade-type bridge over an oozing burn.

Giffnock knew many of the same sorrows and hardships, fears and distresses of the Second World War as the rest of Britain: the rationing and the War Office telegram; the scream of air raid sirens and the threatening roar of enemy planes on their way to targets more important than a rural village-suburb like Giffnock. But on one of the May nights of the Greenock blitz in 1941 (only a few weeks after Giffnock families had taken in refugees from Clydebank), a 'stick' or group of bombs fell across Giffnock on Percy, Eglinton, Hathaway, Berryhill, Stratton and Arden Drives and Avon Road. There were no serious injuries but two houses (one each in Hathaway and Percy Drives) were destroyed. Later, two new ones replaced them, and it is easy to observe now the difference in style between them and neighbouring homes. These pictures show one of the devastated houses and the start of reconstruction of the other. Rebuilding and repairs were paid for by a government department called the War Damage Commission.

The 1939/45 war was over. Young veterans were returning from service looking for comradeship and cheerful activity at home to help them integrate into peacetime life. Giffnock, like other places, offered interest groups and social clubs, and this concert-party of ex-service folk and students was one of them. Among them were the ex-POW, the decorated and wounded, the Normandy landing soldier, the army nurse. This group gathered considerable talent and, during these resettling years, produced regular musical events and dramas, presenting their efforts in the Orchardhill hall in Church Road (and further afield in Scottish Community Drama venues). Close friendships and several marriages resulted from club life; one or two went on to work in the professional theatre or in the BBC; and the group pianist Robert Sutherland later became accompanist to Maria Callas. Another performer was James MacTaggart, later an award-winning television producer. Photographed here are:

Back row: Matthew Blair; Archie Leitch; Robert Sutherland; Ian Moultrie; Nell Somerville; Ian Law; Stewart Montgomery.

Front row: Pearl Taylor; Hazel ___; Sandra Moultrie; Dorothy Gibson; _____; Anna Law; Nancy Yuille; Sheila MacLellan.

In the first century of life at Giffnock station, whistles blew, red and green flags waved and trolleys were piled high with holiday trunks. Little plots of garden blossomed along the platform in summer and fires crackled in the waiting-rooms in winter. By the 1960s that heyday was past, however, and station surroundings were bare and utilitarian until Hughie Lambie arrived as porter. He had lost an eye in an accident and wore a black patch. The other eye twinkled, and dozens of travelling schoolchildren loved the pirate-like porter, who supervised them boarding and leaving the trains. In a more innocent age, he handed out photographs he had taken of groups of them in their school uniforms as they clattered over the railway bridge humphing their school satchels.

Picture reproduced courtesy of the Daily Record.

Hughie felt for all his passengers. He found a discarded three-piece suite and a table and installed them beside the fire he had relit in the waiting room. Rail managers objected and Hughie lost his job, or was at least banished from Giffnock. There was uproar among his young friends. A petition was organised, and for several frantic days children and adults rallied round to sign, as in this picture. The cause appealed to all the train-users, the press appeared, and Hughie was reinstated – although the easy chairs weren't!

A comprehensive aerial shot of most of the north of Giffnock as it appeared in the 1930s during the early days of the pre-Second World War housing expansion. The view from the bottom left of the picture shows everything north of the Orchard House Hotel, with Orchard Drive, Barrland Drive, Dalmeny Avenue, Arnside Avenue, Burnfield Road, the railway line and the houses within that grid. Beyond that lies the area that became Braidbar Nurseries and the site of the Carlton Gate houses. On the right-hand side lie the semi-villas of the curiously empty Fenwick Road and the houses of the short Edwardian May Terrace (c.1911) across the railway. Back on the main road there is the police station complex and the sweep of Braidholm Road through the half-built Merrylee Park Estate. In the top-left quarter lies the empty, hedged farm field awaiting the Tudor Cinema, built a few years later. Lying parallel to Fenwick Road (then Kilmarnock Road) are Elliot and Rowand Avenues. Halfway down Elliot Avenue and behind the cottage, later demolished to add shops to the existing row, can be seen a tennis court and the remains of outbuildings belonging to Orchard Farm.

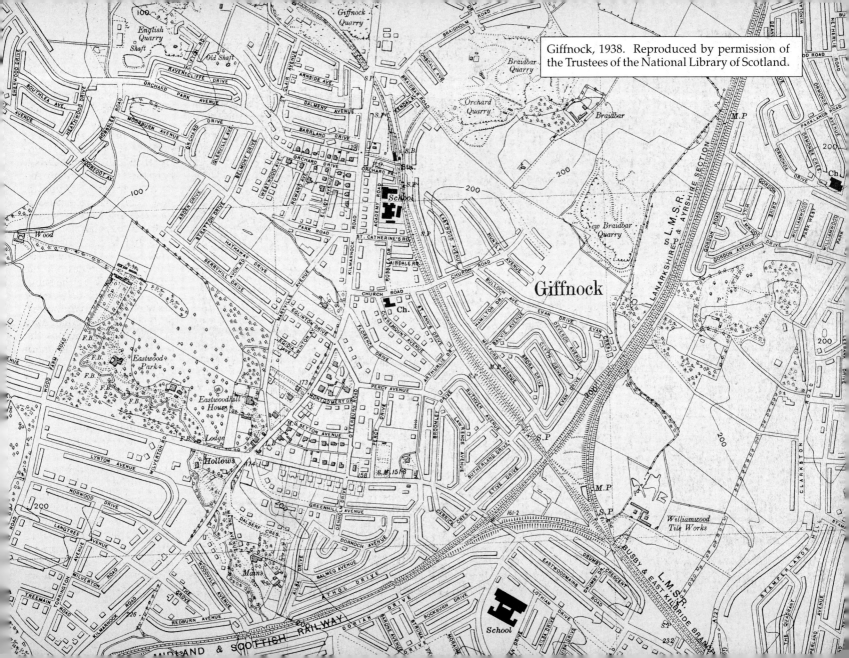

Although this terrible accident at the Busby Road shops took place in Clarkston, the calamity which killed more than twenty people and injured over 100 deeply affected the entire area. Giffnock families felt the same shock, pain and grief following the disaster of 21 October 1971, and share the tragedy as part of their history. Accumulated gas in the basement of a central row of shops on the north side of the road caused a massive explosion. It brought the cars left on the roof car park crashing into the shops below and threw aside shoppers like rag dolls. Efforts by police, firemen, nurses, doctors and others from major incident services were quick and effective, rescuing, evacuating, comforting, and making safe the dangerously overhanging mass of concrete and tangled metal. There is little left now, except a plaque, to tell the tale, but those local residents of then and now rarely pass the scene without a shudder.